WHITE CHICK

WHITE CHICK

NANCY KEATING

ELIXIR PRESS

DENVER, COLORADO

WHITE CHICK. Copyright © 2021 by Nancy Keating.
All rights reserved. Printed in the United States of America.
For information, address Elixir Press, P.O. Box 27029, Denver,
Colorado 80227.

Author photo: Lonna Sullivan
Cover art: Allyson Uttendorfer
Book design by Steven Seighman

Library of Congress Cataloging-in-Publication Data

Names: Keating, Nancy, 1953- author.
Title: White chick / Nancy Keating.
Other titles: White chick (Compilation)
Description: First edition. | Denver, Colorado : Elixir Press, 2021. |

Summary:
"Winner of the Elixir Press Antivenom Poetry Award"-- Provided
by publisher.
Identifiers: LCCN 2021020900 | ISBN 9781932418767 (paperback)
Subjects: LCGFT: Poetry.
Classification: LCC PS3611.E2425 W48 2021 | DDC 811/.6--dc23
LC record available at https://lccn.loc.gov/2021020900

ISBN: 978-1-932-41876-7

First edition: 2021

10   9   8   7   6   5   4   3   2   1

CONTENTS

Threads

Sightlines

I had no idea it was going to take this long.

JUDY CHICAGO

INTRODUCTION

Nancy Keating's *White Chick* races through self-doubt, dubious prayer, politics, and shame, pausing to dwell on the serious topics of race, class, and presidential administrations (both past and present). It's unlike most poetry collections that focus on such weighty issues, though. The sassy and irreverent tone keeps the pace fast, and the cultural commentary speeds by, though it always hits its mark as it goes.

The titular poem comes first, a list poem about, as might be expected, the "white chick" who is the "implied narrator" of both this poem and the entire book. This poem is by turns funny, self-deprecating, and sad, but it's also completely self-aware of privilege. It's also intelligent and doesn't shy away from the silly, even superficial: shopping and its joys cannot be ignored. The "white chick" who once lost herself "in the pages of decorator magazines," however, also "gets really pissed whenever politicians send women to the back of the line, which / seems to happen a lot." The tension between these two positions governs most of the book—and drives it forward.

Prose poems punctuate all of the sections, and they almost act as brakes on the intensity of the narrator's constant self-examination, though many are marked—and slowed—with internal slashes, as though to indicate traditional line breaks. "Thoughts and Prayers" does this, and it blends the journalistic and the meditative in a beautiful way. The obvious allusion in the title is referred to in the sentence "We live in a country of tormented boys," but thoughts and prayers also lead to the grim word- and mind-play of "missing mass is a mortal sin / mass killing is a mortal sin / except in wartime."

The long sequence of petitionary prose poems is particularly noteworthy, as they shift ground from prayers to "Sister Magpie: Matron Saint of Materials" and "Saint Spangle: Matron Saint of Embellishments," both of which celebrate the arts of knitting, to the "Prayer to Saint Melania: Patroness of Trophy Wives," which is a slightly wicked, though also rather tender, send-up of the subject.

White Chick is unabashedly feminist in its subject matter, and it takes on many examples of patriarchy, from the celebrity of Hugh Hefner to the irony of the seeming joy of the "Blonde in an Updo, Dancing," who is angling to "marry a man with a title (yes!)." The poem about Judy Chicago's "The Dinner Party" is titled "Networking," which subtly recalls a line from "White Chick": "white chick used to have focus and networked like hell and joined professional organizations and / took classes and dressed for success." The line is followed by "white chick would have liked to be important."

Of course, any introduction to a book titled *White Chick* would be incomplete without at least mentioning the obvious fact that the "implied narrator" and the book's dominant imagery are studies of whiteness: white dots, a snowy egret, salt, the poem titled "Whiteness" that riffs through every line on the color. Given the history of race in the United States, some readers may find this troubling. And I confess that, as a white woman myself, I struggled with this issue—and with choosing a book as the winner of a contest that was clearly written by another white woman, though I did not know who she was. And yet, I kept returning, with pleasure, to the intelligence and the humor, the downright honesty of the poems and the playful use of metaphor and detail. The poems of *White Chick* are funny, timely, and, best of all, self-aware, a refresher course on language in this time of the partisan platitude and the tossed-off tweet. I could not resist them.

Sarah Kennedy
contest judge

FAULT LINES

white chick

white chick has a lot of obsolete skills

white chick colors her hair

white chick had four immigrant grandparents

white chick didn't play with Barbie

white chick wants to fit in

white chick never really liked her body

white chick identifies as cisgender and hetero and knows how boring that
is

white chick's career consisted of lateral moves

white chick only ever wanted a girl

white chick would like a platform

white chick never wanted to take a man's name but uses her father's

white chick tallied up 18 instances of sexual abuse in her life

white chick is not a plot device

white chick is so white even sunblock doesn't help

white chick grew up in a suburban subdivision about which the less said
the better

white chick remembers New York before it was glossy

white chick used to think when a man hit on her it was her fault

white chick uses chick ironically

white chick checks her privilege

white chick knits to calm herself

white chick has considered body augmentation

white chick never really got the fine line between pressure and seduction but hey, it was the '70s

white chick checked all the boxes

white chick watches the news and drinks red wine. the worse the news the more the wine. so much wine.

white chick sees female news commentators, plural, at last, and is so glad

white chick catches herself judging the commentators, their hair, their makeup, their curation of accessories

white chick carries decades of anger

white chick doubts her progress

white chick is so sorry for being white

white chick always thought Black men were so much more polite than white men but now she thinks she knows why and she wants to apologize for that too

white chick is ashamed at her lack of physical courage

white chick gets really pissed whenever politicians send women to the back of the line, which seems to happen a lot

white chick doesn't get why she hears her own voice apologizing so often

white chick (let's admit it) thinks getting pedicures is creepy

white chick didn't have mentors but she did attend two universities that gladly took her parents' money

white chick hopes it isn't all hopeless

white chick used to lose herself in the pages of decorator magazines

white chick is ambivalent and lacks focus

white chick used to have focus and networked like hell and joined professional organizations and took classes and dressed for success

white chick would have liked to be important

white chick wasn't sure whether to be the shit or marry the shit

white chick gives excellent karaoke

white chick could have been a contender

white chick knows status shopping is a trap but sometimes she does it anyway

white chick is your implied narrator

White Dot

Dear Silicon Valley,
              You don't mind, do you,
 if I leave my phone at home
while I dash out to the dentist
or the library or rally or airport—
after all, why should you care
about my boring life—
I'd only be a white dot
moseying down the artery—

and besides, in the library
I only look things up—
not check them out—
that would leave a record
of my interests
for you to sell to advertisers.

I must confess,
sometimes I click on an ad
for real estate in Missoula—
or a guns-n-ammo show
in the city. Swap meets.
I'm just funnin' ya.

It's to get back at that biometric
face of mine you've got
from every public place
I've been to. I kept meaning to
do my hair.

The Snowy Egret

Give me another word for regret,
             something more like *forget*
                         only better, more effective,

since in fact we really don't forget
             the bad things we did
                         or caused. I read in a letter

to *The Sun Magazine* where a man
             will always remember the egret
                         lying, a silent heap of cirrus clouds,

at his 12-year-old feet. It was his first
             and last time shooting a gun.
                         His confession stabbed me

into a memory of unremembered shame
             and the ache in my stomach telling me
                         I had joined humanity.

String Theory

Does it mean something when you read to the end
of a story and realize you remember nothing? Is it
bad, should you mind that long threads of thought,

so attenuated, pass from the screen to your
eyes to your mind, then gone? Right through you like
coffee. What could this mean, the strand that enters

and leaves and unravels and spins away? Think of a sweater
in reverse, sleeves taken off, its stitches undone, fiber
devolving to down on the underside of a goat in Tibet.

There used to be a rock song, demonic or plain incoherent
when they played it backwards. (If it was country music
you got your job back, your dog back, your darling back.)

Benjamin Button: he rewound totally, to gone.
I unwind someone else's poem, mining it for words.
A cake does not unbake. An egg does not unhatch.

Fault Lines

the astronauts are dying / or should I say passing / people die / cars pass
on the freeway / disturbed teen boys take guns to school and kill a dozen
people / how does a body look with three bullets in her torso / and
somebody hurt our president's feelings again / oh brave new world / these
days I hope for the sky to stay empty / I miss the majesty of looking up
/ my dreams are all commercial / like perfume ads where I'm the starlet
in the gown / younger and thinner / always younger and thinner / in the
morning we get up and drink coffee / and scan words and images with-
out comprehension / the picture of dead children in the water / the child
in the airport seat with someone else's blood on his face / I tore out his
photo / found it again on my desk / but it feels so long ago / where do I
put it / when will I feel the love again / half of us live in a flood zone /
the rest in a dust bowl / or on a fault line / one way or another / the earth
swallows us all / unreasoning sadness piles up like old tires / the homeless
billionaire who slept in five-star hotels / came to rest in LA / he lay down
in penthouses / mother earth will swallow you / they found him before
he began to smell

Actually, It Is All About Appearances

The looming apocalypse has started
to interfere with my shopping, I realize.

Stress gives me hives; unattractive.
I rely on that opinion leader *Vogue*

and strategize ways to accessorize
dread. It's a compromised world order:

skanky new sheriff on the rise,
devising new ways to monetize power,

a white-wearing wife who plagiarized
her address to the voters who, rather than

analyze anything, instead scrutinized
her Slavic eyes and slim dress size.

And while she glamorized theft,
her husband euthanizes truth

and demonizes rivals, wiser voices,
anyone daring to criticize.

Now, she weaponizes five-inch heels
while fashion designers polarize:

will they politicize their label
or say goodbye to a White House prize?

I'd see a name I despise on dresses
every time I walked into Lord & Taylor—

did anyone realize how the election
would colonize retail? *Quelle surprise.*

Erasure

after "tropos" (1993) by Ann Hamilton

After all those years of silencing a woman does it to herself; on vellum, in burnt umber pencil, yet. Let's postulate an artist, excluded from the in-crowd of boldface names, takes a sacred text, excises every word, then blows it up and hangs it. Could be Vasari's *Lives of the Artists.* Could be *The Painted Word.* Could be Scripture. Who can tell? It's been obliterated. Sacrilege! A woman should have respect for the canon. I've been informed the art world's an incestuous market, where "inclusive" means including the artists who are well-known already. Given the disintermediation of the monied class, the tangibility of art seduces investors palming their devices to check on the latest prices at Christie's. I know, obliteration is a trope. Preemptive strikeout, another trope. To vilify sexism under the oligarchy, trope trope trope. In her public shutdown, how loquacious the conundrum she presents.

Playboy of the Western World

I see by my phone that Hugh Hefner is dead
and Amazon puts the new *Playboy* at $12.99

it's about to be Halloween and for $45 I could buy
a Playboy bunny costume from Walmart

Pornhub's slowly killing the empire
and the clubs shut down long ago
but licensing the image of prey
will finance the way forward

the Playboy mansion sold for $100 million
but it's only money

Mr. Hefner paid $75,000 to sleep next to Marilyn forever
it seemed important to him
her ripped-off centerfold made him
she's alpha and omega

but any playboy will deny it's about the money
sometimes it's the thumb-your-nose conviction
that you landed in a tedious family in error
switched at birth for an international icon
and you were destined for loucher things

a pipe   a Lamborghini or three   a mansion
with a grotto and a private zoo
a closetful of pajamas for most occasions

a set of blondes for every photo op
and each blonde with a set of big girls

Hef was a hoaxer with the big story
killing the uptight father again and again
such a squaresville man
with his soul-killing responsibilities

only Daddy-O isn't dead
he comes back over and over to ask
what's the point of the black satin sheets
the lacy panties gathering dust on that chandelier
now the lifestyle's viral

the leader of the western world sizes up any woman he sees
(so long as they're white)
and there are men proud to announce
they're entitled to only date babes with sizable racks
and women blow tip money on boob jobs
and insist up and down that they love threesomes
and practice smiling while talking
since even now degrees hardly matter

the poet listed and Googled words deployed in the *Times*
pornography   playboy (lifestyle)   café society   womanizer
jet set   male chauvinism   hedonism   pimp   paparazzi
premarital sex   sexual revolution   boys club   rape culture

online you'll find the picture of the archivist
who looks after a roomful of black leather books
documenting Hef's every move and utterance
in clippings that meander in from all compass points
his job secure indefinitely

Blame

Drive anywhere and
you see a highway shrine,

its wilting wreaths
and cross and teddy bears

a proxy for people's grief
and need to show the world

where someone they loved
gave up the ghost.

They're not here anymore.

What you do see is a lone
tree outed as a killer,

naked but for damp trinkets
on a February day,

marked out among the thousands
of trees on miles of road.

Thoughts and Prayers

I tumbled headfirst off the cathedral roof / and that felt like no dream /
We live in a country of tormented boys / I would have prayed for the bird
who sings no longer / my mother would have prayed for the boy who
shot the egret /*imprimatur* / the word in the front of some religious books /
means *print it* / and *nihil obstat* / *nothing hinders* / I don't feel my prayers find
an ear / too many narratives / special interests / good fences / My beau-
tiful mother / who is dead now and knows everything / does she know
how hard I tried to be good / was trying / I know I was trying / still do
/ it's always boys who do the shooting / do things for no reason / just to
do / knowing this / would we go back / could we have sung the bird back
to life / I'm not good enough / to make a miracle / Once at mass I took
communion in a torn-off corner of a missal page / they said girls couldn't
sing in the choir / I wished I could be bad enough to make a spitball / I
swallowed it / only boys could sing / byzantine religion / missing mass
is a mortal sin / mass killing is a mortal sin / except in wartime / unless
it's not a just war / a term to be sliced and diced / medieval theologians
debated how many angels could dance on the head of a pin / why should
God hear a prayer of mine / when every Sunday I stay home and sin again
/ I'm sure I bore the elders / they're easily bored / my dreams are so often
interrupted / everything we tell them they doubt / maybe I'm boring
God / and the angels sing

How to Look Believable★

No shirttails. No rich-looking blazers.
Go with the turtleneck.
Wear the beat-up loafers;
cover up. Dark colors. Avoid
the sleeveless anchorwoman look.

Later you'll be interviewed
on the nightly news.
You're the plaintiff,
the accuser,
the expert witness,
the one who wrote that
11-page document
everyone's quoting.

Here's the subhead
in the Style section:
Sometimes all you can control
is what's visible on the outside.

Yes to double denim. No
to the top that puts a little midriff
on display, or maybe it was No
to the flowered Banana Republic skirt.

If you're a broke grad student,
be sure to look the part,
but also like a grown-up.
If you never wear makeup,
don't put it on now.
Always put your hair up.

Remember the hearing
will last six hours
and most people in the room
hope to trip you up.
You'll be telling strangers,
mostly male,
about your drug use,
dating history,
public episodes of hysteria.

Next they'll be telling us
how to pack a bug-out bag.

* Source: The New York Times, January 4, 2018; by Eva Hagberg Fisher

How to Save the World

after "Weltrettungsprojekt" [World Rescue Project], 1995-ongoing,
Vanda Vieira-Schmidt

In Germany, in an asylum, there lives a woman who makes art. She is
free to make art all day every day as much as she likes, because they say
she is crazy. On her moderate days, maybe she says so too. In any case,
all day she draws sketches for the secret police to decode, for the protec-
tion of the people of the world. She loves the people of the world. She
is doing this for them. I think I know how she feels. In California there
was an heiress who believed she'd die if her mansion ever was complet-
ed; the workmen kept adding crazy little rooms and windows and stairs
to nowhere and were still working on it when she died. There are times
when I'd like to live in an apartment building where all my neighbors are
old friends, and there's a dining hall downstairs, and a laundry service so
that all I do all day is sit here and write. Sometimes I believe if I'm good
enough I might make a small difference, put off terrestrial catastrophe just
a little longer, although between her and me we're definitely creating our
way through a lot of trees. This lissome German woman has lent her desk
to an art exhibit. It looks like a tidier version of the desk I am using right
now. I suppose she's back in Germany making more drawings to save the
world, and she'll add them to this burgeoning mountain of office paper
when they bring her desk back to her. Ezra Pound was committed to an
asylum for shooting off his mouth, saying he admired the way Mussolini
ran Italy. Stupid effete Fascist. Crazy like a fox, though—there he was
in the asylum, central heating, no bills to worry about, all kinds of time
to write. He did some good work in there. Remember "step on a crack,
break your mother's back"? We kids were very careful on the sidewalks.
A coup topples one bad government in favor of another one. Mosquitoes
kill millions of humans and livestock, but Donald Trump is fine. Some-
how he got in and I'll be put away. This is what happens, what they do to
you, where they put you.

Whiteness

the right kind of migrant. white. birthright. white. reliance on license to terrorize. white. irish draft riots. white. apologizing for buying souls as chattel. white. "I sing myself and celebrate myself." white. ellis island. white. de facto apartheid. white. redlining. white. fires at midnight. white. eye for an eye. white. quiet trials at night. white. Dwight Eisenhower court fight. white. freedom riders. white. flight. white. striving stymied by. whites. miller time. white. higher education. white. high-tech, science, finance. white white white. literary lions mostly male and. white of course. a rising tide lifts all boats, says JFK, but mainly. white people. pliable and quiet. Nikes. white. blood diamonds to delight who? white women. slice and dice and parse and gerrymander. white. michael jackson? lighter. lives lost while driving while not white. busted tail lights and nonfunctioning cop cameras and bystanders filming with their phones. witnesses.

I Didn't Mean To

See my father nude (just for a second).
Break the cordial glasses.
Lose my first real love.
Backtalk my mother.
Minimize my privilege,
ignore the beauty, complain
too much, know so much; ask
all the rude questions and still hope for approval.

Do any work today.

Look down on my whole life.
Trash organized religion. (No, actually,
I did mean it.) Worship at bad altars.
Glorify designer labels. Get raped.
Spend too much, obsess over
unattainable men, watch that blowjob.

Waste time. Spend too long in the Midwest.
Avoid having children.
Have so little impact.
Marry late and wrong.
Question the science. Laugh
when my boss got fired.
Let my mother die alone.
Fall in love with pinot noir.
Telegraph my ambition.
Lie about the price of my shoes. Make nothing happen.

Irish Pubs

The marketing mavens of Guinness
for years have sold pubs in a box,
shipped to publicans across the globe.

Unload the crate for instantaneous patina.
Banners, bats, old pipes, harness brass,
the paraphernalia of an actual pub,
where the peasantry and Ascendancy
might have shared a pint in the day,
giving trinkets to the landlord.

No trouble at all to round up the stuff
from dusty shops in the countryside.
Pack it and ship it away,
just like the Irish millions.

I spotted my grandfather in Siena once,
in sepia with a row of other lads
wearing the uniform of a team, Grandpa
with his long limbs and untroubled brow,
his hand, holding the ball, intact.

Hawaii

There's a fire in the boatyard across the street,
and my husband wakes me up at 5:15 to tell me this

in the grey of gradual waking from silver dreams
and hands me my first mug of coffee and we stand

at the second-floor window, ringside seat,
while the trucks pull up, seven, and two hook-and-ladders

squirm their way into the boatyard driveway—
the back way to the row of shops that's burning.

No one lives there, so it's a show in dovish hues,
black char of peaked rooves hard by a lava of flame.

The second-guessing: why does it take forever
to screw the hose to the hydrant? why do the men

seem to amble and discuss? is there a hose
in the cherry-picker? shouldn't there be trucks around front?

Tongues lick out, holy, from the ash-grey roof—
they tear at the seam of a normal morning, my mind informs me,

sees a picture in my missal of the apostles at Pentecost
and we wonder if it's gotten to the paint store yet.

Someone sets a row of orange cones to block the street--
streams of water hit the roof and dissipate--

the scene is blocking the smoky dawn and a glow
surrounds the noncolor neutral of suburban real estate

and I think how the palette reminds me of Kiliwaia
on film, its lava orange and sparking and surging

over its blackened mountain as far from us as could be
and still America ... joggers and walkers with dogs and coffee

pause, like the way we watch the evening news
and its faraway deaths, drinks and knitting in hand.

The Problem with Gratitude

Not to get all Debbie Downer on this, but
the problem with gratitude is that it's such a should,
meaning my life is so great I don't get off complaining
about anything at all. Oh, I know I should be grateful
for being married to a mensch, despite the fact that he's
deeply eccentric – as in, he wears a fakey yacht-captain cap
while capsizing his catboat because, guess what, he's
a bad sailor, which he'd be the first to tell you. So he calls 911
and the entire South Shore bay patrol, and a couple of
village cops and Good Samaritans come to save him. Hello.
The bay is mostly three feet deep. Did he tell everyone
he's married to me? Of course he did.

At least now and then we get an invitation to something
where I can wear a cocktail dress. I'm grateful for that.
So, gratitude. I guess deep down I'm shallow. Thinking
about fashion when refugees are spilling out of rafts.
I can't think about that. Where's God in all that?
What can I do? I watch the news and boom, I'm complicit.
I'd march, but there are never enough bathrooms.
See how ungrateful I am, always saying "but" instead of
"and." Bring on the self-flagellating guilt. Something I'm
really good at. Not sure if this is a gift I should be grateful for.

You don't really want to go around being grateful--
it's kind of Facebooky, kind of braggy, like that parable
where the Pharisee thanks God he's so successful and generous
while right there next to him, the bar owner begs the Lord
over and over to forgive him and the point of this story,
as Jesus asks us rhetorically, is who does God like better,
Mister Smug or Mister Humble? I think we know.

Critical News

Here's the news for today:

Denim is the iconic American garb,
known the world over.

We all need a moto jacket.

Pastels will be strong this spring.

The model has $90 socks on.

From the page to the gaze
to the brain
then out again,

the input competes for meaning.
Headlines tell me women fight back
wearing black. I try to square this
with the awareness of white,
a photo of an army of models
in white suits and gowns,
as an echo of the suffragists.

Please, someone,
give me the color of the day.

A Moving Attic of Memory

after untitled "environment" in "and then leave me to the common swifts"
by Kai Althoff

In frustration, flipping through the exhibit handout
at MOMA, you look for the name the artist
might have given to the stuff in the large vitrine.

There is none. Yet it touches you; here are
the scraps of your grandmother's bureau drawer
(minus the scent of sandalwood sachet)
where she kept gifts too good to use:

gold braid, velvet ribbon, antimacassars,
old words for old things. The crocheted lining
in the bassinet. Purses they called reticules

at a life stage we now label vintage,
in other words older than obsolete
and therefore chic. Look,

here's an atomizer from a perfumier just like
the one I gave Nana, and spoons for salt
and demitasse. Nobody spoons out salt now.

We live in homes with no dank rooms
and in our compulsive locomotion we'd never
hear a murmur of memory, if indeed there was one.

The artist's goal: the negative palliative,
the null hypothesis. His "Solo for an afflicted trumpet"
has no trumpet. He changes installations every time.

Interviewer: What do you want to be remembered for?
Artist: I don't want to be remembered.

Tearsheets in the Inspiration Pile

A wedding announcement
that says the couple played together as babies,
and met again as adults
at the wedding of the groom's brother.

Someone else's poem that says
poetry is stupid and she wants to die.

Titles of poems and pieces
in the scrap pile:
Acorns, Quahogs, Blame,
Identity, Strange,
The Tavern Parlor.
One of them uses the word "Luciferian."

A nine-paragraph wedding announcement
paid for by an aristocratic couple
which lists all their parents' achievements
and their own
as well as both families' memberships
in the Society of the Cincinnati.

An obituary for an English codebreaker
who worked at Bletchley Park
and helped sink the *Bismarck*.

A product list from the pharmacy
of Santa Maria Novella in Florence—
all in Italian, of course,
in a typeface I recognize
from my diplomas,
an oversized sheet of paper

that I had hoped would conjure up
the gilded elegance of the shop itself.

Subject matter of tearsheets in the pile:
pinwheels. Pollen. Monty Python.
The flora and fauna of the Hempstead Plains
(killdeer, mullein, timothy grass).
Fairy tales. The fanboy way my father loved
the actress Madeline Carroll;
he painted her from a movie still.

A fragment of a poem about
the sports I won't take up,
the men I won't take up,
the vices I won't take up,
the life's work not pursued.

She Screams with Laughter

after "El Morocco, New York" (1955) by Garry Winogrand

Say she's a Rob Roy kind of woman;
that, and steak, bloody. She wouldn't go
for lobster; such a gold-digger thing to do,
go for the costliest thing on the menu,

besides which, lobster is messy
and she wants to be sleek, tonight
of all nights. She is dancing for her life.
Her life could be exactly as glamorous as

this ephemeral nanosecond, but only if
she plays him right. No time for dithering,
we're not getting any younger here
and life without a man is harsh.

A hypothetical investigator might ask
for proof that the picture wasn't posed
in a studio. You can say it's El Morocco.
Who's to say it's not the Copa, the Stork,

the back room of a Second Avenue dive?
On the activity: is that a peabody or just
perambulation, dancing or a hug?
Moreover, is her partner some plank or patsy

or someone she can contend with for
a decade or three, or four? The camera blinks;
a bark of laughter, tooth and nail.
Whatever he said was hilarious. Say it.

If We Had Had Our Say

Cathedral doors would open like flowers.

The Eiffel Tower would be
a bowl of filigree.

Coal would stay inside the mountain.

Handknits would cost more than
emeralds.

Museums would overflow
with male nudes
by female artists.

Carpooling would be an Olympic event.

Vacuum cleaners would run silent.

So would leaf-blowers.

So would motorcycles.

Cleavage would go out of fashion.

Spinning

I never remember
what "numinous" means

spider spins a high wire home
her how is her what
this teetering practicality

every thread the result
of a void leaped over

she doesn't think
she sizes up
though every leap is lower

she weaves a gossamer gravity
that shimmers in the rain
grey gray gris grizzled

spinning her arachnid story
where she lost the promotion

she got above herself
the gods put her in the same old job
dropping down to darn tears

THREADS

Knitworld

Spider fingers, he calls them   fingers I use for picking lint
bipolar husband calls out hyperactivity   there's a headline
don't try to stop me   knitting is my anthem
each row a song   each cardigan a symphony
every skein a cocoon in the making   the throughline of my life
doing the things women do   mostly   controlling the result
don't look for economic value   that's a ranking game from
the world where   a nose to the grindstone gets you a short nose

Mary made a seamless tunic for Jesus   a technique not a miracle
knit for a hundred hours and you too can attain divinity
we in knitworld sing our potential   we hold up our work
to a chorus of praise   in knitworld we have no trail of bodies
and to misquote Saint Tom Hanks   there's no crying in knitting
you don't need to be lucky   or make sure the office door stays open

Prayer to Sister Magpie
Matron Saint of Materials

Dear Sister Magpie, whatever I can cast on or wind up, help me make of it a thing of funky originality. Let not any scarcities of conventional yarn stop me. Grant me the vision to see what can become of old cassette tape, the odd shoelace, the bits of ribbon saved from Christmas presents, my grandmother's frugal ball of recycled string, the plastic bags ripped into strips, fishing line, dental floss, gardening twine, and even spools of electrical cable. Oh Matron Saint of Materials, bestow on me also the gift of time so that I may knit 24-7 in a parallel life even as I satisfy the demands of others on me, and grant that I may never do violence to another using tensile piano wire, but instead knit it up into a small kitchen appliance or something similar.

Amen.

Prayer to Saint Spangle
Matron Saint of Embellishments

Dearly beloved Saint Spangle, you of the sequins and baubles, the feathers and pompoms, give us the imagination to see what small household objects might be incorporated into these drab offerings we create for our loved ones, especially my friend Alice, who is allergic to wool and only wears understated colors. Grant us the persistence required to thread the pearls and beads, all 700 of them, onto the boring cotton yarn I must use to quickly make Alice a scarf, yet another goddamned scarf, excuse my blasphemy, for her birthday which is right around the corner. Through your intercession with Jesus, who both you and Alice are on better terms with than I am, guide me as I make Alice something beautiful and fun, that Alice may wear it and rejoice during one of her innumerable daily visits to her fragile 94-year-old mother, who has tired of living but can't let herself die and may drag Alice down with her. Dear Saint Spangle, I praise your love of flashiness. Together may we channel that love into a happy accessory.
Amen.

Prayer to Saint Melania
Patroness of Trophy Wives

Oh glamorous Melania, you of the slashing cheekbones and smoldering eyes, while you may not be canonized yet--for that one needs to be dead, actually—I thank you for your contributions to the heightened renown of knitting, though I know it was far from intentional. I read in the *Times* where you knitted navy-blue sweaters, more than one, as a young girl in Sevnica, your charming Slovenian nowheresville of fewer than five thousand souls. You and your girlfriends passed notes between houses on strings of yarn, notes about the boys you might marry or love (big difference) and what the webs to ensnare them might be. The article mentioned navy-blue sweaters, plural, and I wondered what was up with that, Melania. Maybe it was to go with your uniform for school. I had a navy one, too. In Google's photo gallery, every picture shows you posing in solid colors. Sleek. I guess you started early. After you gave that speech you cribbed from Michelle, the white dress you were wearing sold out. You favor white dresses, I see--kind of like a uniform for a bride. I like to see what we find noteworthy and what is passed over. To me, a sweater is the starting of something, an entire garment made from a single thread. In a way, we make ourselves. Melania, show us your navy-blue sweaters, your starter ensembles. We need something that won't unravel, these days especially.
Amen.

Prayer to Saint Isidore
Patron Saint of Animal Husbandry

Oh Saint Isidore, through whose care and dedication we fiber addicts find it possible to score handspun natural undyed yarn at the farmers' market on Saturdays, please grant a long and virile life to Richie, the black ram whose nappy patch of fleece I scratched last Tuesday while visiting a sheep farm upstate. Richie and I had a moment, Saint, him with his wide intelligent hazel eyes, regarding me across the chasm of unrelated mammals. He ate the grass I offered; he ate the grass in his pen. It was all the same to him. Like you, he does his part, Saint. You roll up your sleeves and muck out the pens, while like a biblical prophet, he knows 40 ewes a year. Patiently he offers up his curly coat to the carder, the spinner, the knitter, the factories of the world, asking nothing more than a field of grass and the occasional rub between his horns. As grows the fleece, so spins the yarn. Black sheep, black roving, black yarn, textured when spun by hand, with traces of lanolin inherent. Pray God for long life to Richie the Wise, and blessings on all his kin.
Amen.

Prayer to Saint Mark
Patron Saint of Lawyers and Notaries

Gracious Saint Mark, evangelist, apostle, and all-around good writer, you who are patron saint of lawyers, notaries, and prisoners—so, basically, the designated protector of those who labor under the constraints of bureaucracy—grant me the patience to sit through the interminable hearings orchestrated by my local municipality to bore the public to death so that, after most people go home to bed, the zoning board may move in favor of the big property owner. Saint Mark, keep me mindful that I, alone in the room, was the only person apart from the developer to accomplish anything, in his case approval of a $20 million deal, in my case half of a glowing gold mohair shawl in the feather-and-fan pattern. (Although, to be fair, that's an excellent suit the council president is wearing, beautifully cut.) I understand that as patron of paper-pushers, you and I might be at cross-purposes, but you are also the patron saint of lions, and who knew magisterial tawny lions prayed? As a civic watchdog, I try to embody the saying, "They also serve who only sit and wait." Who said that, Saint, and were they serious? Please tell me which side you're on.
Amen.

Prayer to Saint Dita Von Graph
Matron Saint of Measurement

Oh Blessed Saint Dita, your shape stays in your memory, your body is
your yardstick, and your wingspan equals your height. Dearly beloved
Matron Saint of Measurement, bless us with the understanding of rules of
thumb, such that a foot measured shall forever be a foot, as is the elbow to
wrist, and help us conjure even from the legally-mandated 100-yard dis-
tance the proper measurements of the former lovers we stalk, that we may
continue to knit them unwanted yet beautiful sweaters and vests, despite
the fact that all this devotion freaked said ex-lovers out and they called us
clingy and codependent and they didn't want to commit themselves to a
relationship right now. Grant that the famous knitting curse be lifted and
that these same ungrateful yet deeply hot former lovers come to see the
error of their ways and return to our wooly embrace. In you, Saint Dita,
we place our trust.
Amen.

Prayer to Saint Joseph
Patron Saint of Cabinetmakers

Saint Joseph, stepfather to Jesus, who raised Him to succeed you in a carpenter's trade, you glow in the window at Chartres, both you and the boy, smoothing a slab of cedar. Please bless my cabinets and trunks and crates, the built-ins that came with the house along with the bureau my neighbor set out at the curb and which I dragged across the street to take possession of in my never-ending quest for storage for my handknits. For while my balls of yarn can remain in their totebags or even rest temporarily, a couple of years at the max, in stackable plastic storage bins, what I make deserves to live in wood. Wood that's planed and drawers that are dovetailed. In butternut, maple and pine. Saint, it's the least they deserve, my bulky demonstrations of love. Some of us keep everything. Look here: I have an old boyfriend who's saved the sweater I made him in college, a grey one with cables. I know because he sent me a picture of it, posed on a hanger, matted in plexiglass. He had someone sew elbow patches onto it, his wife, I expect. So there it was, an elephant in the middle of somebody else's marriage. Saint Joseph, please inspire him to give it a drawer, and a rest after all this time hanging.
Amen.

Prayer to Saint Meridel
Matron Saint of Lefties

Oh, radical Saint Meridel, you who told the interviewer that victimhood made all women fearful, and who admitted you were always intimidated and afraid, the beauty is that no one could tell from your books. Help me face and overcome the dread. For I do have dread, and have been a victim, a word I disdain. Saint, I have tried to live life with my head down, but even in knitting, my differences show. My cables twist left instead of right. When I follow a pattern precisely, the buttonholes wind up on the man's side. I don't want to be a man; I just covet their birthright. I find security in knitting circles, safe places where no man deigns to enter. Short of more self-defense classes, we all know the rules: backs to the wall, knives out. In our case, needles and scissors. Saint Meridel, you who lost your house because the FBI suspected your leanings and their watchfulness kept driving lodgers away, console me in my anxiety, which sits deep inside me and ranges over many subjects, physical to financial. At 3 a.m. I lie awake under my mother's afghan, restless with the common womanly terror of finding herself alone in an unfamiliar meadow, no one knowing where she is, concerned that some stranger might happen along. Oh saint, let me not show weakness. Help me throw out the rulebook.
Amen.

Prayer to Saint Lydia
Patroness of Dyers

Oh alchemical Saint Lydia, first-century stirrer of cauldrons of flowers
and leaves, give us this day the orange fiber from the skin of red onions,
the miracle of indigo, the tawny earth of walnut husks, and please refrain
from reminding us that sometimes the truest shades can wash out and
fade like a memory. Saint Lydia, you know first-hand what can come of
the lowliest weed. I'm thinking about the happiest yellow of any field of
dandelions, our yard, the yellow ink they made on a playsuit I had then. I
lay on my stomach among them, this field of gold, like coins, like the pet
canary my father named after a Swedish tenor, among the bees, air-hang-
ing and dusted with pollen. And that was the end of the playsuit, the
stains no mother or miracle-working detergent could remove, stains like a
rapturous sin. Now I boil the blossoms and brew an amber tea, then scoop
out the flowers and throw in the hanks of wool. Then stir. Then steep.
Then drain and rinse and there it is again, the yellow of morning in June.
Saint, I want to make love to the yellow, eat it and drink it and bathe in
it. Yet all I have in my hand, really, is three hanks of yarn. It's like the
potential for love, Saint, or genius. We dream it into our reach. Then we
awake and it fades like a color in the sun. Saint, we want it back.
Amen.

Prayer to Sir Thomas More
Patron Saint of Politicians

Your Grace, you may find this an odd request, but my knitting guild really needs guidance. It's been hijacked by a new president, and you would not believe the palace intrigues and pot-stirring we've got. Once upon a time, Sir Tom,--may I call you that?—our guild was a utopian place where women sat peaceably and knitted and chatted and did all the things the haters laughed at us for and not always behind our backs, but we were happy. We organized bus trips to alpaca farms. We made chemo caps for cancer patients and hats for the veterans. Then our longtime president, who had some family issues, decided not to run for another term. Donna raised her hand and volunteered, so she was elected. She held it together till May, and then she brought the crazy, telling Group A that Group B looked down on them, accusing half the board of being against her in an email that went to the whole membership. Sir Tom, ours is a small empire, but she's got a two-year term. People are skipping meetings. People say they're quitting. Execution isn't an option, sadly. We're thinking of a coup. We're looking for a loophole. What do we do? What would you do? Amen.

Prayer to Saint Maureen
Matron Saint of Irish Knitters

Say it ain't so, Saint Moe—may I call you Moe? that's what we call my
aunt Maureen—! I've been reading secular books that say the Aran Isle
sweater was the creation of some branch of the Irish tourist board. Skewer
my Celtic pride! Growing up in the blandest and flattest of suburbs and
the newest of houses, still I was an Irish lass, complete with the requisite
freckles and naturally-curly hair. And tribal forces conspired to bring the
Clancy Brothers albums into the house, each showcasing a row of men in
their cream-colored pullovers. All Ireland all the time. Saint Moe, I spent
school afternoons learning to knit while Mom and I sang along to "The
Gypsy Rover" and "Four Green Fields." Half my schoolmates had Irish
names. When the nuns got new habits, we thrilled to see Sister Franny
X was a redhead. We taught each other jigs and reels in the playground,
if nobody brought the jump-rope. And now I find the Clancys were
nothing more than stage Irishmen whose agent bought their wardrobes.
My ethnic faith is shaken to the core. Next you'll tell me the Irish eat
their young. No, wait—that was an ex-friend of my parents', and she was
speaking for herself, the way hers turned out. Pardon me. Pardon me all
to hell.
Amen.

Prayer to Saint Acrylius
Patron Saint of Synthetics

Oh beloved Saint Acrylius, you who was favored by Woolworth's and
Newberry's and Lee Ward and so many five-and-dimes of yore, please
shine your light on my request to God for forgiveness for my long-ago sin
of making and giving all my friends those knitted (but mainly crocheted)
vests and headbands and bags and whatever else might be trimmed with
fringe or macramé in those dreadful DayGlo back-to-the-earth colors so
current back then, so humiliating now, looking through these fading or-
ange Polaroids--although, to be fair, Saint, when one is young and lovely
no stratosphere of tackiness in wardrobe can truly succeed in making
your radiant health ridiculous. My old friends grin and glow, shoulder
to shoulder, so high and happy in their Seventies orangey-gold-avocado
acrylic granny-square vests, with their muttonchops and Afros and ironed
Peggy Lipton curtain of hair. Those nasty vests, so pilled and matted,
would outlive us unless one were to be torched by the spark of an errant
reefer. So many of us, in our marijuana hazes and our literature seminars,
smiled like sunsets back then, Saint. Some are no longer with us, Acry-
lius. If you see them, apologize for me, and say I knew not what I was
doing.
Amen.

Prayer to Saint Reversaline
Matron Saint of the Do-Over

Oh patient Saint Reversaline, I need to tell you, you are the knitting saint I find most difficult to pray to. Yet, I believe you alone would understand my dilemma. I just ripped out an entire boatneck sweater, right up to the neck, because that's where the problem started with this thing. Call it original sin. People who pray, and even the rest of us, know all about original sin, the idea that you don't even start out perfect, and it's down-hill from there. So if that's the case, why should anyone even bother? The yarn only cost me $20. For that, I could get online and order myself a cotton striped boatneck pullover that channels Audrey Hepburn at her most appealing, with that swanlike neck she had. (My mother used to envy *my* swanlike neck. She is gone. No one else ever took note of my neck.) But no. I can't bring myself to put a bad sweater in the trash. It's not the sweater's fault I put the front and back next to each other and both sleeves on the same side. I was too hasty. I failed to embrace the process. Saint, if you would, guide me to that zen state I should be getting from these sticks and string.
Amen.

SIGHTLINES

Cats

after Barbara Guest

The simple contact with a wooden stoop and the cat
recovered herself, began to stretch as fur, forced
as she stood crouching to consider the fortitude where
feline looked at foreign invasion, where lizard brain
lumps me in with the pterosaur and wild boar, cat
readying to give as good as she gets. Catholicisms
of predator and prey scamper up and down the alley
in Chartres, the dead-end kind the French call an *impasse*,
bon mot, and all the cats in the sand-colored houses
all attached, no spaces between them, a style
of house whose name I could not put my finger on,
have arranged themselves in their respective windows
to watch the wordless soundless ruckus of my standoff
with the gray tabby my avid isolated self
had hoped to caress. She spotted me at 20 meters
and took up the species of crouch which no amount
of my ignoring her would get her to abandon. Her inscape
told her to do it, it was Animal Behavior 101. My map
showed me the church of St. Pierre on this side, which
turned out to be closed. It wasn't my catechism
that told me to seek out any tiny church in France,
only the hope of a catapult of surprise: the wood-painted
vault, the categorical madonna not in any guide.
All the same, she disappointed me, this cat,
this excuse for a delay in rejoining my travel partner.
I would have stroked her belly. She would have purred.

Networking

after "The Dinner Party," 1979, by Judy Chicago

We do it all the time and here we are,
trolling around the banquet table
checking out the names at every place.

Every teaspoon, every placemat
a triumph of the needle arts (a gentle slap
to critics who undervalue women's place)

has been set with its own exquisite
ceramic vulva-motif molded dinner plate,
Each resting secure in its appointed place.

Never seen so many monumental names
of famous women no one's heard of,
so many vulvas in one public place.

There needs to be some infinitesimal
sorting here, a reverse exclusivity;
So many women didn't get a place.

I can hear the conversations now
across the centuries, what this one
might have done in that one's place.

Blonde in an Updo, Dancing

*after "Miss Marian Seymour dancing with Baron Theo Von Roth at
the Grand Opera Ball, N.Y.C.," 1959, by Diane Arbus*

Perhaps she is bored. Could be
she's in some abracadabra reverie—
marry a man with a title (yes!),
just the right key in the ignition
to rev up your fastidious
humdrum life. Quick: jump-start
the round of photo-op parties, bring on
the armsful of kooky size-2 friends.

Or not. The man is a high-toned
party planner, hired by the hotel
to revive its ailing nightclub. He took
the title himself, playing with variations
on his name. Fair play to him,
giving Miss Seymour the spotlight.
She had to angle hard for that hairdo;
Kenneth was booked for weeks ahead.
How angelic she seems, a sleeping
child, not remotely calculating
as she sashays in the Baron's arms,
playing her part impeccably
in the brevity of one festive night.

Opportunity Cost

The deals we don't make sometimes count the most.
At her garage sale, the elderly woman and I
evaluate each other. "Jennifer's son is an investor
in Florence," she tells me. For a dollar, I negotiate

a fake-Lalique spray bottle of a perfume
whose valuation peaked thirty years ago. "You have
your mother's lips," she says, then: "My brother
had a crush on your mother" back then,

in Queens with every Catholic ten-year-old a startup
attending grammar school at Mary Gate of Heaven.
I can imagine my mother's indulgent smile
as she walks home along Liberty Avenue,

daydreaming her own balance sheet. The boy grew up,
moved west, invented the fax machine. He hosts
family reunions on his compound, endows charities
in high-need global sectors. "He'll be so thrilled

when I tell him," she said, tell him she met
the daughter he didn't have with the woman
whose cool youthful due diligence led to
a null class of non-events, non-monetized bliss.

Dolls, Boxes

after Joseph Cornell, "Untitled (Bébé Marie)"

women calling the home shopping channels
will mainline their CZ earrings from QVC   with Easy-Pay®
those two twinkling eyes   winking up from the aqua box

the brunette model will be pointing to her earlobes
blinking like a satiated cow
        her whole being becalmed   a sort of Xanax joy

and Lisa the hostess will say three thousand pairs
                are sold already
but if I pick up the phone I won't have a moment   of disappointment
"Get the something you didn't get on your special day   you to you"

MarlysHeatherCarol can't get to the mall
        the chemo tires her out
her mother is dying in the next room
her man doesn't understand   the transformative whatever
of jewelry

Lisa will say "Thank you so much for the call   MarlysHeatherCarol"
"aren't you glad you shared   have a blessed day"

they just arrested some woman in the Bronx   her daughter is
terminal
she embezzled a million from the archdiocese
                to buy collectible dolls
the cops packed up 20 crates of toys   in their original boxes

if you change one thing about yourself

you will trigger a transformation   says
Lisa

Baby Marie   looks out through a twig forest
            in a Joseph Cornell box at MoMA   the old bisque doll
with her chipped nose   sober glass eyes open forever
            made outside Paris   loved in Brooklyn

decades ago her owner paraded her in a stroller
Midwood Street to Flatbush Avenue   Maple to Nostrand   with
pride and care
            Baby Marie took a spill once   the girl rocked her and cried
and stroked her hair

Imitation: Murmur

after Bruce Smith

After the jets crashed into the buildings and the buildings
telescoped down like a pair of ancient mariners at attention or
malfunctioning accordions pleating the air and the brother
of a grammar-school classmate I used to know, I remember him,
red-haired, freckled, big teeth, was one of the bond traders in
that company that lost most of its people, I thought how my cousins
were both Marines, both working in the Pentagon, but the plane hit
one of the other four sides of that building, not T.J.'s wing, and Peter
was away. My aunt, marooned in Ireland visiting relatives, called
the embassy to check on me and they did. I told the disembodied
dulcet Irish voices on the phone to let her know that. Grateful, yes, but
surprised that embassies had all that time to make personal calls on behalf
of a nun from Long Island. I should carry more gratitude in my heart.
I'm never grateful enough to be alive, to live here in America,
but sometimes I wonder. The next year didn't I go to Ireland and
saw the same relatives and weren't they asking me about the president
and the troops. Then we invaded Iraq, again, and Peter went in
the second time too. He's a career man. He looks like Tom Cruise, with
stamina to burn. I have a photo of me and my four cousins,
one rose of Sharon and four pin oaks, all Republicans. You go to war
with the army you have, Rumsfeld said, another shameless empty suit
at the podium with a catchphrase for the ages: great way to approach dat-
ing after the divorce, after the parents died in stereo and then the planes
hit. Look in the mirror. There's your arsenal. We've all consecrated to this
aggrieved mindset. It follows us close by like a retinue. Oh, my heart—
they tell me it's a murmur, I say it's a metaphor. I pass the treadmill test.
Sisyphus could easily have been a woman, we really know from tedium.
But I feel ashamed sometimes. My country bombs the Middle East
with mendacity, not occluded, mendacity right under your nose, there

for anyone to see, unlike the weapons of mass destruction which actually
were not. What we did have was soldiers mocking prisoners, taking
naked pictures with piss, shit, jism, humiliation. Whose lives were
diminished to make mine as good as it is? My big problem is loss
of looks or health; another is procrastination. They tell us we're safe
because they've got an eye out, or they tell us we're not safe because
who knows? It's like a virus, everyone lying, presidential candidates
on down, bad airbags but they cover it up, bad pipes in the schools
that they knew about, bad health studies because some company
paid the scientists, our values tanking like hedge funds. Everyone
wants to get over. After 9/11, my office got a tip that some locals
were beating up the clerks at the 7-Eleven, that the cops were there
and the paper should cover it. I called the cops. Never happened,
they said, no story there. I should have known better. After the towers
were built I hated them, so tall you could see them on a clear day
from Robert Moses beach. But on that day, you could watch them burn,
a pair of candles, then only the smoke pulsing from 40 miles west.

Always One Foot Out the Door

Once a friend of mine shared a rumor
of someone's uncle   who kept
thirty fully packed suitcases
in a locked room   for his friends

always keep a passport
and a getaway bag

Suitcase Man had been a refugee
a professor   impeccably dressed
in the old style
from Istanbul or Trieste

always leather shoes
always polished
people like this still roam the earth

I think of the wandering Aengus
grown old and disheveled
out on one road and the road beyond it
chasing a memory of delight

Last night at the Indian restaurant
our friend showed us
his passport   he carries it everywhere

I look over at you

The Road Is My Middle Name

from the Bonnie Raitt songbook

they say Louise was not half bad   right down the line
an angel from Montgomery standing in the doorway

I can understand why a woman must have an outside man
since I fell for you I'm blowing away   I got plenty

I'm a mighty tight woman   run like a thief
let's give 'em something to talk about

everybody's crying mercy
I want to take you on a slow ride

been too long at the fair
when I met you on the Midway

you've been in love too long
write me a few of your lines

what is success   everything that touches you
are you ready for a thing called love

you told me baby   you used to rule the world
give it up or let me go   you got to know how

come to me   guilty   tangled and dark
cry like a rainstorm and howl like the wind

ain't gonna be your sugar mama no more
I can't make you love me   luck of the draw

about to make me leave home boy
my first night alone without you   walking blues

if you won't love me why don't you let me go
one part be my lover one part go away

Weekday Evenings on the Belt Parkway

after "Purple Wind" (1995) by Alex Katz

Just after sunset, I would see
dusk bruising like a plum
and it's not farfetched to feel
Mr. Katz saw the same things I did
in the eternal gloaming of
childhood, parents discussing
in the front seat of the Rambler,
me looking out the side windows
at the apartment houses rushing by,
sometimes seeing people inside
with their glowing lamps
at dinner, or in their loungers,
or during their card games,
cozy and home for the evening
the same as we soon would be,
and that violet of the blue hour
was a refreshing place,
a place where these window people
loved or at least cared for each other
(our car on the parkway pushing east
so quickly they were only a blur,
but I loved all their lights on),
where the bare tree in the side yard
that leaned away from the wind
leaned toward at least some of
the people who had incubated it
from an acorn, prayed over a wishbone
that it would grow, and planted it
exactly there.

Orange as in

the flesh of the cantaloupe / as in carp in a pond / as in a president's
pompadour but I see lately he's going blond / as in the cheeks of the
male Australian finch / as in a sunset seen through pollution / as an
astronaut's jumpsuit / as in the real color of a black box / as in whatever
henna touches / as in a pair of goldfish / as in the final blinding flash /
this is only a test / as in sensation / as in Norman-Irish white-chick hair
/ as in a Buddhist monk burning / as in a torch lighting a church / men
in suits are standing at podiums / as in mango and papaya and tangerine
and persimmon / wipe out the sink with the dishtowel of reality / as in
a rust-colored chrysanthemum / so many tints and shades / as in a pris-
on jumpsuit / as in desire and pain / as in the flap of the bogman's torso
under glass in Dublin / as in the Sunshine State / as in carrots for eye-
sight / as in the father's ultimate hospital bracelet / as in hazard cones
around a catastrophe / as in fire / as in hell / the world intrudes on the
farmers' market / orange as in foxes flashing past the corner of your eye
/ as in Pentecostal flame and prayer and tongues of inspiration above the
apostles' heads / as in pumpkins for children to practice their carving
on / so we can make our own monsters /as in the visible air above the
refineries in Jersey / as in Good Queen Bess's hair in the Armada portrait
/ as in the jellyfish that entrances through thick aquarium glass / men at
podiums declaring none of it is true / orange as in the rising full moon
in December / as in the roots of an invasive vine we pulled in the yard /
as in heat / as in whatever made the alarm go off

J. Peterman Is Selling Grandpa's Police Whistle for $30

The way men once used to say
they read *Playboy* for the articles,
that's how I read the J. Peterman catalog,

my reality surrendering to reverie,
lost in novelistic product descriptions
name-checking distant places and times,
in watercolor illustrations that idealize
a line of blazers, caftans, fascinators

--a fascinator results from the illicit love
of veil and headband--.

J. Peterman plays me like the uilleann pipes,
giving my consuming self
an education the way Peter Sarsgaard
gave Carey Mulligan *An Education*
in that movie. (Well, only sort of.)

Gobsmacked shock,
cool steel in my fingers and mouth:
The no-doubt-sherry-drinking
catalog copywriter notes that
the police whistle here on offer
is the real deal made by J. Hudson,
the very one London bobbies used.

J. Peterman needs you to know
its goods are all about authenticity.

I resist buying it. I used to own
the one Grandpa had from his days
when the Irish police answered
to London. He quit the force
and then he fled the country.

Now his granddaughter,
a fully assimilated suburban white chick,
doesn't need another pendant.

Forces

She said *radioactive isotopes* in the salon
and it started me off. Not every day does

a phrase like that come up in a cellphone chat
but I'm getting my roots done, hostage to

the incessant chemical fountain of youth and
Samantha's on her smartphone between clients

and now she *can't believe* someone's 45
and *ohmigod, John's 51?* Sam is asking

the other someone *where the hell*
does the time go, as I count down the minutes

to Done on this timer ticking next to me.
I'm starting to feel like Dorothy

in that movie as the Wicked Witch of the West
cackles *my pretty* to her and her eyes bug out

watching the sand trickle down the hourglass.
Judy Garland was so young then, and really

so young when she died, pretty much worn out
and now the shampoo girl says to her friend

and all the angels, my God, I tell you, and now
this salon, pink and black as a donut on a

sign in the night, is suddenly consequential
and divine and the isotopes whisper

encouragement to the unseen stranger, 45,
and her slightly older husband and I feel

the rustle of Dante's nine orders of angels
(though only the lower orders bother

with mortals) as lifesaving treatments are
cycling through their ecstatic half-lives of mercy

and heroic forces within us unite with forces
imposed by some outside agency, barely discerned.

Salt

1.
After the water receded, salt stayed in the soil;
it killed the fig tree. That's symbolic,
I'd say.

2.
There's a way to make your own
from ocean water. You need a filter
and cheesecloth. You need to have
no life.

3.
You can taste the salt in blood.

4.
You can taste salt in tears.
I was only sure my father loved me
when he was near death
and could only make happy sounds.

5.
When the water receded,
the salt in the lawn looked
like melting snow. The soil,
parched, refused nourishment.

6.
Blood, sweat, and tears.
Salt, salt, and salt.

7.
After the assault,
the woman felt disgust
at the taste of
her own sweat.

8.
It's a lost form of cruelty,
putting salt in the wound.
We've come a long way
since then.

9.
There's a walled city in France
that prospered during the centuries
of the spice trade. Nowadays
we mine salt, and the village
tells tourists about its storied past.

10.
Ever see a salt sculpture?
Over time, particularly
if the climate is damp,
it will come to look
like the monuments
on Easter Island.

11.
Salt, pros and cons:
Enhances flavor (pro).
Boosts blood pressure (con).

12.
Once salt was money.
Now money is money.

13.
Remember what happened
to Lot's wife?
Before looking back, think.

The Dream with My Mother

"But how do I know you're my mother?" I said.
"You need to take it on faith," she said.

In the shadow of the bedroom, I blanched a bit,
undone by the look of this looming figure
at the foot of the bed. But there was my mother, arrayed

in a broad red cape like the Infant of Prague, though
instead of her beloved face I saw an indigo mesh
in the dusky center of a full-body Nigerian mask.

"How are you doing, my sunshine?" she asked.
"Sometimes I miss you so much," I said.

She wore strips of every drape and slipcover
she'd made for the house on Alwick Avenue,
pieced together in the afterlife of my dream.

She sounded just like herself. I longed to share
that secret smile we had, but when Orpheus
looked into Euridice's eyes he wrecked it for all time.

"I'll never love anyone more," I told her.
"I came to tell you something," she said.

Dinosaurs Among Us

after an exhibit at the American Museum of Natural History

Mounted on an exhibition wall I see
a vestigial bone or rather, a card of bones,

translucent wishbones of 13 kinds of birds
circling that of *Tyrannosaurus rex,* the progenitor,

like the immaculate surround of saplings
born of the central sarsaparilla tree.

The furcula. It holds a sacred place
in wakeful childhood, granting the well-behaved

the permission I was forever prone to seek;
and even then, the wish was purely binary:

big half, small half, yes/no, fervent hope
fulfilled or dashed. I found it best to make

desultory wishes I didn't care about.
And looming in the center of that life

the overpowering overhang of grownups,
listing all the powers I'd never have

until maturity, or decades enough that I might
pretend to that exalted pinnacle.

How did I get here? That dino bone, leaden
and bogged, gave way to twittering birds.

My Life Was the Size of My Life

(title after Jane Hirshfield)

You could say the same about yours.
I don't know what to do with truisms anymore,

given that A equals A, the mathematical reflexive
property, the place philosophers go right after

I think, therefore I am. These days time
is my conundrum and contradiction. I am

rich in time, out of time, time is flying even as
today stretches out toward evening, the biggest

question of all: when will my time
be over, what trivial activity will get interrupted.

Should I go get coffee? Should I just eat a goddamn peach?
Small questions shove aside the larger, the ones no one

can help with. The hottest columnist of my
New York youth uses a walker now. The old lady

at the train station tries to suck me into conversation.
She walks with a four-footed cane. I try not to tell

my future in her pink-rimmed eyes.
Young women are too beautiful in this city.

Saturday morning, and East Midtown walks
with sunglasses and a cup from Starbucks.

All these pedestrians have excellent posture.
My time is limited. I don't know what to do first.

ACKNOWLEDGMENTS

The author is grateful to these publications, which accepted the following works:

The Carolina Quarterly: "My Life Was the Size of My Life"

The Gettysburg Review: "Opportunity Cost"

Long Island Quarterly: "J. Peterman Is Selling Grandpa's Police Whistle for $30"

New Letters:

"Prayer to Saint Isidore, Patron Saint of Animal Husbandry"

"Prayer to Saint Mark, Patron Saint of Lawyers and Notaries" (also reprinted by *Poetry Daily*)

"Prayer to Saint Meridel, Matron Saint of Lefties"

"Prayer to Sister Magpie, Matron Saint of Materials"

Poets to Come (an anthology): "The Problem with Gratitude"

Potomac Review: "Dinosaurs Among Us"

The Southampton Review:

"Prayer to Saint Acrylius, Patron Saint of Synthetics"

"Prayer to Saint Dita Von Graph, Matron Saint of Measurement"

"Prayer to Saint Lydia, Patroness of Dyers"

"Prayer to Saint Maureen, Matron Saint of Irish Knitters"

Southwest Review: "A Moving Attic of Memory," "Always One Foot Out the Door"

TSR Online: "How to Save the World"

Tar River Poetry: "String Theory"

2 Bridges Review: "white chick"

NANCY KEATING's poetry has appeared in *New Letters, Poetry Daily, The Gettysburg Review, The Southampton Review, Southwest Review,* and elsewhere. A two-time Pushcart Prize nominee, she has an MFA from Stony Brook University and teaches at Farmingdale State College.

ELIXIR PRESS TITLES

POETRY

Circassian Girl by Michelle Mitchell-Foust
Imago Mundi by Michelle Mitchell-Foust
Distance From Birth by Tracy Philpot
Original White Animals by Tracy Philpot
Flow Blue by Sarah Kennedy
A Witch's Dictionary by Sarah Kennedy
The Gold Thread by Sarah Kennedy
Rapture by Sarah Kennedy
Monster Zero by Jay Snodgrass
Drag by Duriel E. Harris
Running the Voodoo Down by Jim McGarrah
Assignation at Vanishing Point by Jane
 Satterfield
Her Familiars by Jane Satterfield
The Jewish Fake Book by Sima Rabinowitz
Recital by Samn Stockwell
Murder Ballads by Jake Adam York
Floating Girl (Angel of War) by Robert
 Randolph
Puritan Spectacle by Robert Strong
X-testaments by Karen Zealand
Keeping the Tigers Behind Us by Glenn J.
 Freeman
Bonneville by Jenny Mueller
State Park by Jenny Mueller
Cities of Flesh and the Dead by Diann Blakely
Green Ink Wings by Sherre Myers
Orange Reminds You of Listening by Kristin
 Abraham
*In What I Have Done & What I Have Failed
 to Do* by Joseph P. Wood
Bray by Paul Gibbons
The Halo Rule by Teresa Leo
Perpetual Care by Katie Cappello
*The Raindrop's Gospel: The Trials of St.
 Jerome and St. Paula* by Maurya Simon

Prelude to Air from Water by Sandy Florian
Let Me Open You a Swan by Deborah Bogen
Cargo by Kristin Kelly
Spit by Esther Lee
Rag & Bone by Kathryn Nuerenberger
Kingdom of Throat-stuck Luck by George
 Kalamaras
Mormon Boy by Seth Brady Tucker
Nostalgia for the Criminal Past by Kathleen
 Winter
I will not kick my friends by Kathleen Winter
Little Oblivion by Susan Allspaw
Quelled Communiqués by Chloe Joan Lopez
Stupor by David Ray Vance
Curio by John A. Nieves
The Rub by Ariana-Sophia Kartsonis
Visiting Indira Gandhi's Palmist by Kirun
 Kapur
Freaked by Liz Robbins
Looming by Jennifer Franklin
Flammable Matter by Jacob Victorine
Prayer Book of the Anxious by Josephine Yu
flicker by Lisa Bickmore
Sure Extinction by John Estes
Selected Proverbs by Michael Cryer
Rise and Fall of the Lesser Sun Gods by Bruce
 Bond
Barnburner by Erin Hoover
Live from the Mood Board by Candice Reffe
Deed by Justin Wymer
Somewhere to Go by Laurin Becker Macios
*If We Had a Lemon We'd Throw It and Call
 That the Sun* by Christopher Citro
White Chick by Nancy Keating
The Drowning House by John Sibley
 Williams

FICTION

How Things Break by Kerala Goodkin
Juju by Judy Moffat
Grass by Sean Aden Lovelace
Hymn of Ash by George Looney
Nine Ten Again by Phil Condon
Memory Sickness by Phong Nguyen
Troglodyte by Tracy DeBrincat

The Loss of All Lost Things by Amina Gautier
The Killer's Dog by Gary Fincke
Everyone Was There by Anthony Varallo
The Wolf Tone by Christy Stillwell
Tell Me, Signora by Ann Harleman
Far West by Ron Tanner